AMERICAN HEROES

ELEANOR ROOSEVELT

Making the World a Better Place

AMERICAN HEROES

ELEANOR ROOSEVELT

Making the World a Better Place

SNEED B. COLLARD III

Marshall Cavendish
Benchmark
New York

For Judy O'Malley,
another true visionary and friend

Marshall Cavendish Benchmark
99 White Plains Road
Tarrytown, New York 10591
www.marshallcavendish.us

Library of Congress Cataloging-in-Publication Data
Collard, Sneed B.
Eleanor Roosevelt : making the world a better place / by Sneed B. Collard III.
p. cm. — (American heroes)
Summary: "A juvenile biography of First Lady Eleanor Roosevelt"—Provided by publisher. Includes bibliographical references and index.
ISBN 978-0-7614-3069-8
1. Roosevelt, Eleanor, 1884-1962—Juvenile literature. 2. Presidents' spouses—United States—Biography—Juvenile literature. I. Title.
E807.1.R48C648 2009
973.917092—dc22
[B]   2008002068

Editor: Joyce Stanton
Publisher: Michelle Bisson
Art Director: Anahid Hamparian
Designer: Anne Scatto
Printed in Malaysia
135642

Images provided by Art Editor Rose Corbett Gordon and Alexandra (Sasha) Gordon, Mystic CT, from the following sources:
Front cover: The Granger Collection, NY
Back cover: Topham/The Image Works
Pages i, 27: Time & Life Pictures/Getty Images;
pages ii, vi, 3 top left & right, 4, 7 top & bottom, 8, 11, 12, 23, 30: The Franklin D. Roosevelt Presidential Library & Museum;

page 1: Library of Congress;
page 3 bottom: Christie's Images/Corbis;
pages 15, 16: Bettmann/Corbis;
page 19: Corbis;
page 20: Private Collection, Look and Learn/The Bridgeman Art Library;
page 25: The Art Archive/National Archives Washington DC;
pages 28, 32: The Granger Collection, NY.

CONTENTS

As a young girl, Eleanor Roosevelt felt shy and fearful.

Eleanor Roosevelt

"Looking back, I see that I was always afraid of something," wrote Anna Eleanor Roosevelt. As a child she was afraid of the dark. She was afraid of upsetting other people. She was afraid to fail. But during her life Anna, or Eleanor, as she was called, overcame her fears. She became First Lady of the United States. She did more for our country than almost any other person in history.

Eleanor lived a lonely childhood. She was born in New York City on October 11, 1884. "I was a shy, solemn child. . . ," she remembered. "I am sure that even when I danced I never smiled." Her parents, though, were very popular. Her mother spent her time going to parties and other social events. Her father enjoyed hunting and riding horses. "I loved the way he treated me," Eleanor wrote. Unfortunately, her father also had a drinking problem. He would leave his family for months at a time.

Eleanor's parents were very active socially.
This left them little time to spend
with their children.

Even though she had two younger brothers, Eleanor felt more alone than ever after her father died.

Both of her parents died before Eleanor was ten years old. After her mother died, Eleanor and her two younger brothers began living with their grandmother, Valentine Hall. "My grandmother felt we should be at home as much as possible," Eleanor recalled. Eleanor was taught by private tutors. Other children rarely came over to play. She passed the time by helping her grandmother's servants do chores. She also spent long hours reading. Books took Eleanor on adventures she could only dream about.

But soon, she would have real adventures.

When she was fifteen years old, Eleanor sailed to England. She attended a school run by a French woman named Miss Souvestre. At the school, Eleanor spoke French. Miss Souvestre liked Eleanor. She took her on vacations through Europe. Eleanor became fascinated with all kinds of people, places, and events. For the first time, she learned what was happening in the rest of the world.

Miss Souvestre's school in England opened Eleanor's eyes to the bigger world.

Miss Souvestre

Eleanor's cousin Franklin liked her intelligence
and the way she cared about other people.

When she returned to the United States, Eleanor was eighteen years old—an age when young women were supposed to look for husbands. This was a painful time for Eleanor. She was smart and had seen many things. She felt, though, "that there was nothing about me to attract anybody's attention." Then, Eleanor caught the eye of Franklin Delano Roosevelt. Franklin was a distant cousin of Eleanor's. He loved her intelligence and how she cared about other people. The two married on March 17, 1905. Eleanor's uncle, President Theodore Roosevelt, gave her away at the wedding.

For the next fifteen years or so, Eleanor looked after her family. "My husband and my children became the center of my life and their needs were my new duty," she wrote. She and Franklin had six children. One of them died as a baby. Meanwhile, Franklin jumped into politics. In 1910, he won election to the New York State Senate. In 1928, he was elected governor of New York.

While Franklin jumped into politics, Eleanor raised their children.

Eleanor and Franklin became a powerful team, especially after he was struck with polio.

Franklin's success in politics forced Eleanor to grow in new ways. No longer could she stay quietly at home, especially after 1921. That was the year a disease called polio struck Franklin down. After that, he could barely walk. He depended on Eleanor to go out and see how America and Americans were doing. Eleanor overcame her early shyness and began talking to thousands of people. She shared what she learned with Franklin. Together, they became a powerful team.

In 1932, Franklin was elected president of the United States. As Franklin's wife, Eleanor became the First Lady. In the 1930s, America was suffering terribly. These were the years of the Great Depression. Millions of people lost their jobs and their homes. With Eleanor's help, Franklin worked to lift the country out of its misery. He began a series of programs called the New Deal.

*It was a great day
in 1933 when
Franklin, with
Eleanor on one side
and their son James
on the other, entered
the White House.*

The New Deal programs got millions of Americans working again.

The New Deal gave money to struggling farmers. It provided help to many other people hurt by the Great Depression. New Deal programs also put Americans back to work. One program was called the Civilian Conservation Corps, or CCC. The CCC hired young people to plant forests, repair damaged farmland, and do other outdoor work. Another program was the Works Progress Administration, or WPA. It hired more than eight million Americans to build highways, bridges, libraries, and other projects.

Eleanor often gave Franklin ideas for New Deal programs. In 1933, she visited coal-mining areas in West Virginia. Many of the miners were out of work. They could not feed their families. Eleanor told Franklin about these terrible conditions. Together, they helped organize settlements where mining families could start over and work as farmers and laborers.

Eleanor's ideas helped ease the suffering of many coal-mining families.

World War II brought new challenges for the nation—and for Eleanor.

Thanks to the New Deal programs, America began lifting itself out of the Great Depression. Unfortunately, another problem was coming—World War II. In the 1930s, both Japan and Germany began attacking neighboring countries. In 1941, Japan also attacked the United States. The United States declared war on both Japan and Germany.

Now Eleanor was busier than ever. She and Franklin met with leaders from all over the world. Every day, for many years, Eleanor wrote a newspaper column. She called it "My Day." Her column helped inform Americans. It gave them courage during these hard times. Eleanor also visited American soldiers and wrote letters to their families. She always worried about what would happen to these brave men. Before the great battle known as D-Day—the day America and its allies invaded Europe—Eleanor wrote: "Soon the invasion will be upon us. I dread it."

Drawn by
MARTHA SAWYERS

I Want You to Write to Me

MRS. FRANKLIN D. ROOSEVELT

THE INVITATION which forms the title of this page comes from my heart, in the hope that we can establish here a clearing house, a discussion room, for the millions of men, women and young people who read the COMPANION every month.

For years I have been receiving letters from all sorts of persons living in every part of our country. Always I have wished that I could reach these correspondents and many more with messages which perhaps might help them, their families, their neighbors and friends to solve the problems which are forever rising in our personal, family and community lives, not only with my ideas but with the ideas of others.

And now I have a department in this magazine which I can use in this way. The editor of the WOMAN'S HOME COMPANION has given me this page to do with exactly as I will; but you must help me. I want you to tell me about the particular problems which puzzle or sadden you, but I also want you to write me about what has brought joy into your life, and how you are adjusting yourself to the new conditions in this amazing changing world.

I want you to write to me freely. Your confidence will not be betrayed. Your name will not be printed unless you give permission. Do not hesitate to write to me even if your views clash with what you believe to be my views.

WE ARE passing through a time which perhaps presents to us more serious difficulties than the days immediately after the war, but my own experience has been that all times have their own problems. Times of great material prosperity bring their own spiritual problems, for our characters are apt to suffer more in such periods than in times when the narrowed circumstances of life bring out our sturdier qualities; so whatever happens to us in our lives, we find questions constantly recurring that we would gladly discuss with some friend. Yet it is hard to find just the friend we should like to talk to. Often it is easier to write to someone whom we do not expect ever to see. We can say things which we cannot say to the average individual we meet in our daily lives.

To illustrate the changing nature of our problems it is interesting to remember that less than twenty years ago the outstanding problem of the American homemaker was food conservation, or how to supply proper nourishment for her family with one hand while helping to feed an army with the other! Ten years ago the same mothers were facing the problem of post-war extravagance and recklessness: how to control the luxurious tastes of their children, the craving for gayety, pleasure, speed which always

follows a great war. Today in millions of homes parents are wrestling with the problem of providing the necessities of life for their children and honest work for the boys and girls who are leaving school.

At almost stated intervals the pendulum swings, and so far the American people have each time solved their problems. And solve them we will again, but not without earnest consultation and reasoning together. Which is exactly where this page enters the national picture.

LET US first consider one or two typical problems. You all know that in May the entire nation celebrated Child Health Week. I was among those who spoke on the basic foundations on which the health of a child is built. A few days after I gave this radio talk I received a letter from a mother who wanted to know how she could supply nourishing food and proper clothing for her three children when her husband was earning exactly fifty-four dollars a month!

Again, a couple who had read something I had said about modern methods in education wrote asking what trades or professions would offer the best opportunities for young people in the next few years.

You will note that both of these earnest letters came from parents. Most of the letters which reach me are from parents. This is encouraging, for there never was a time when the sympathy and tolerance of older people were more needed to help the younger people adjust themselves to a very difficult world.

In the hands of the young people lies the future of this country, perhaps the future of the world and our civilization. They need what help they can get from the older generation and yet it must be sympathetically given with a knowledge that in the last analysis the young people themselves must make their own decisions.

You will be reading this page in midsummer when discussion of the summer vacation is paramount in many American homes. I am an enthusiastic believer in vacations. They are, in my opinion, an investment paying high dividends in mental and physical health.

So this month I am going to ask you a question. We all know that we have less money to spend on recreation than we have had for a great many years. How can we make that money cover the needs of a real holiday? I should like to have those of you who have taken holidays inexpensively tell me what you have done.

Perhaps you will be interested in a holiday that I myself enjoyed many years ago.

We took four young boys to whom we wanted to show some points of historical interest, at the same time giving them a thoroughly healthful trip. We decided to take our car and strap on the side of it one big tent

and one pup tent. The four boys slept in sleeping bags with their heads under the pup tent if it rained. We ran about one hundred and fifty miles a day. We would buy our supplies in some village through which we passed in the late afternoon. Then we would make camp near some river or brook, usually finding a hospitable farmer who would supply us with milk, butter and eggs.

We had to cook our supper and make our camp before it was dark, after which we would have a swim and sit around, talk or read and go to bed in the twilight. We were up again at dawn and during the day we would stop and see whatever historical things might be of interest on the way. Our route ran north through New York State so that we saw Ausable Chasm, the shores of Lake Champlain. We stopped a day in Montreal and two days in Quebec; then we drove down through the White Mountains where we camped two days in order to climb some of them on burros, to the great joy of the children; then east through the beautiful central part of Maine with its lakes and woods, down to the sea to Castine, and home by the road along the shore.

Our actual camping trip lasted ten days and cost us only the wear and tear on the car, the gasoline and oil, and our simple food, with a very little extra for admissions, for donkeys to climb the mountains and the cog railway up Mt. Washington, but these of course could have been eliminated. This was one of the least expensive holidays I have ever taken and it could easily be duplicated with profit and health for all concerned.

A LESS elaborate trip may prove quite as satisfying. A week or two in a good camp has its advantages if swimming, fishing and hiking are available, and even week-end picnicking will break the monotony of summer in city or small town.

If you have taken such a trip with family or friends, won't you tell me about your experiences, giving sufficient detail to serve those who wish to duplicate your vacation? Your plan may be just the one I should be glad to pass on to other COMPANION readers.

Please do not imagine that I am planning to give you advice that will eventually solve all your problems. We all know that no human being is infallible, and on this page I am not setting myself up as an oracle. But it may be that in the varied life I have had there have been certain experiences which other people will find useful, and it may be that out of the letters which come to me I shall learn of experiences which will prove helpful to others.

And so I close my first page to and for you, as I opened it, with a cordial invitation—I want you to write to me.

By writing for newspapers and magazines, Eleanor helped Americans feel that their government cared about them during hard times.

Even during the worst days of the war, Eleanor never forgot about everyday people. In the 1940s, black soldiers were still second-class citizens. Their equipment and housing were not as good as those of white soldiers. They were not allowed to do the same jobs in the U.S. military.

At that time, too, when men were away at war, millions of women worked in factories. At first, they also were not treated well. Again and again, Eleanor spoke out for better treatment of women and black people. Her words made a difference. By the end of the war, black soldiers were allowed to serve in almost all parts of the navy and army. Factory owners set up daycare centers for children so that mothers could work more easily.

Eleanor helped make it possible for women to work in the factories that produced the things America needed to win the war.

There's work to be done and a war to be won ...
NOW!

SEE YOUR U. S. EMPLOYMENT SERVICE
WAR MANPOWER COMMISSION

On April 12, 1945, President Franklin Roosevelt died of a stroke. Harry Truman became the new president, and Eleanor moved out of the White House. A few months later, the United States and its allies claimed victory in World War II. The long war had finally come to an end! Eleanor felt sad that her husband did not live to see that day. She told her daughter Anna, "I miss Pa's voice and the words he would have spoken."

But Eleanor's own work was far from over.

The entire nation mourned for Franklin when he died in 1945.

After Franklin's death, Eleanor became active in the United Nations.

After World War II ended, Eleanor kept writing for newspapers and magazines. In 1945, fifty countries joined to create the United Nations. The United Nations, or UN, was formed to help promote peace, justice, and prosperity for all the world's people. President Truman asked Eleanor to represent the United States in this new organization. As part of the United Nations, she fought for equal rights for all people everywhere. She traveled to every corner of the globe. Her visits built friendships between other nations and the United States. President Truman called her "First Lady of the World."

Even when she was older, Eleanor never stopped trying to make the world better.

As Eleanor grew older, her children urged her to slow down. She wrote, "I am willing to slow down, but I just don't know how." Indeed, she continued to travel, write, and give lectures past her seventy-fifth birthday.

Anna Eleanor Roosevelt died on November 7, 1962, at the age of seventy-eight. Until the very end, she never lost her interest in the world and other people. She never stopped trying to make the world a better place. Today, more than forty years after her death, she is still one of the most admired Americans of all time.

IMPORTANT DATES

1884 Born Anna Eleanor Roosevelt on October 11 in New York City.

1892 Mother dies; Eleanor begins living with her grandmother.

1894 Father dies.

1899 Begins school in England.

1905 Marries Franklin Delano Roosevelt.

1916 Gives birth to last of six children.

1921 Husband, Franklin, struck with polio.

1928 Franklin elected governor of New York.

1929 The stock market crashes; the world is plunged into the Great Depression.

1933 Becomes First Lady when Franklin becomes president of the United States.

1935 Begins writing daily newspaper column called "My Day."

1941 The United States enters World War II after the Japanese attack on Pearl Harbor.

1945 Franklin dies.

1946 Begins serving as U.S. representative to the United Nations.

1948 Helps draft the United Nations' Universal Declaration of Human Rights.

1962 Awarded her thirty-fifth honorary college degree.

1962 Dies in Hyde Park, New York, on November 7.

Words to Know

allies Nations that have joined together to achieve a common goal.

dread To fear something greatly.

First Lady The wife of the president of the United States.

Great Depression A time in America during the 1930s when many businesses failed and many people lost their jobs.

invade To enter another country by force.

New Deal President Roosevelt's plan to end the Great Depression.

polio A disease caused by a virus that attacks the spinal cord. It often paralyzes its victim.

politics Anything to do with running for office or holding office in government, or trying to influence decisions government makes.

prosperity Success, especially in having money or wealth.

second-class citizen A person who is not treated fairly and equally.

solemn Gloomy or very serious.

state senate A group of elected people who help make laws for a
state government.

stroke A sudden sickness caused when a blood vessel that carries
oxygen and nutrients to the brain is blocked off or bursts.

To Learn More about Eleanor Roosevelt

WEB SITES

The American Experience:
   http://www.pbs.org/wgbh/amex/eleanor/
The Quotations Page:
   http://www.quotationspage.com/quotes/Eleanor_Roosevelt
Franklin D. Roosevelt Presidential Library and Museum:
   http://www.fdrlibrary.marist.edu/index.html
   http://www.whitehouse.gov/history/firstladies/ar32.html

BOOKS

Amelia and Eleanor Go for a Ride by Pam Munoz Ryan. Scholastic Press, 1999.

Eleanor Roosevelt: An Inspiring Life by Elizabeth MacLeod. Kids Can Press, 2006.

Our Eleanor: A Scrapbook Look at Eleanor Roosevelt's Remarkable Life by Candace Fleming. Atheneum/Anne Schwartz Books, 2005.

A Picture Book of Eleanor Roosevelt by David A. Adler. Holiday House, 1995.

PLACES TO VISIT

Eleanor Roosevelt National Historic Site
4097 Albany Post Road
Hyde Park, NY 12538
PHONE: (845) 229-9115
WEB SITE: **http://www.nps.gov/elro/**

Franklin D. Roosevelt Presidential Library and Museum
4079 Albany Post Road
Hyde Park, NY 12538
PHONE: (800) 337-8474
WEB SITE: **http://www.fdrlibrary.marist.edu/index.html**

Franklin Delano Roosevelt Memorial
Ohio and West Basin Drive SW
Washington, DC 20004
PHONE: (202) 426-6841
WEB SITE: **http://www.nps.gov/fdrm/home.htm**

Index

Page numbers for illustrations are in boldface.

A Note on Quotes

One of the remarkable things about Eleanor Roosevelt is how she found her voice. After being shy and withdrawn as a child, she developed into a skilled speaker and writer. She left behind thousands of articles, letters, and speeches full of her wisdom and thoughts. Most of the quotations in this book come from her autobiography, published in 1961. I hope they encourage readers to explore Eleanor's remarkable words and ideas for themselves.

—Sneed B. Collard III

About the Author

SNEED B. COLLARD III is the author of more than fifty award-winning books for young people, including *Science Warriors*, *Wings*, *Pocket Babies*, and the four-book SCIENCE ADVENTURES series for Benchmark Books. In addition to his writing, Sneed is a popular speaker and presents widely to students, teachers, and the general public. In 2006, he was selected as the *Washington Post*—Children's Book Guild Nonfiction Award winner for his achievements in children's writing. He is also the author of several novels for young adults, including *Dog Sense* and *Flash Point*. To learn more about Sneed, visit his Web site at www.sneedbcollardiii.com.